Feelings

Happy

Sarah Medina

Illustrated by Jo Brooker

Raintree

www.raintreepublishers.co.uk
Visit our website to find out more information about **Raintree** books.

To order:
☎ Phone 44 (0) 1865 888112
📠 Send a fax to 44 (0) 1865 314091
💻 Visit the Raintree Bookshop at **www.raintreepublishers.co.uk** to browse our catalogue and order online.

First published in Great Britain by Raintree, Halley Court, Jordan Hill, Oxford OX2 8EJ, part of Harcourt Education.
Raintree is a registered trademark of Harcourt Education Ltd.

© Harcourt Education Ltd 2007
First published in paperback in 2008
The moral right of the proprietor has been asserted.

Editorial: Dan Nunn, Cassie Mayer and
  Diyan Leake
Design: Joanna Hinton-Malivoire and
  Ron Kamen
Picture research: Erica Newbery
Illustration: Jo Brooker
Production: Duncan Gilbert

Originated by Modern Age
Printed and bound in China by
  South China Printing Company

ISBN 978 1 4062 0635 7 (hardback)
11 10 09 08 07
10 9 8 7 6 5 4 3 2 1

ISBN 978 1 4062 0642 5 (paperback)
12 11 10 09 08
10 9 8 7 6 5 4 3 2 1

British Library Cataloguing in Publication Data
Medina, Sarah
Feelings: Happy
152.4'1

A full catalogue record for this book is available from the British Library.

Acknowledgements
The publishers would like to thank the following for permission to reproduce photographs: Bananastock p. **22B**, **C**, **D**; Getty Images/Taxi p. **22A**; Getty Images/photodisc p. **12**, **17**,

Every effort has been made to contact copyright holders of any material reproduced in this book. Any omissions will be rectified in subsequent printings if notice is given to the publishers.

Contents

Some words are shown in bold, **like this**. They are explained in the glossary on page 23.

What is happiness?

Happiness is a **feeling**. Feelings are something you feel inside. Everyone has different feelings all the time.

sad

happy

angry

4

When you are happy, you feel good.
When you are happy, everything
seems wonderful.

What happens when I feel happy?

When you are happy, you may feel like grinning from ear to ear. You might laugh out loud.

You might feel like spending time with someone you love.

Why do I feel happy?

Being told you have done well can make you feel very happy!

Playing with friends can make you happy. Spending fun time with your family brings happy feelings, too.

Is it OK to feel happy?

Happiness is one of the nicest **feelings** there is!

When you feel happy, you should enjoy it!
Your happiness can make other people
happy, too.

11

What can I do when I am happy?

You can show your happiness in lots of ways. Jump up and down, or run around outside.

Tell someone you are happy. Give someone you love a hug. It is great to share your **feelings**.

Will I always feel happy?

Feelings change over time. You might be happy now, but then something might make you feel sad.

You can help yourself feel happy again.
Try reading a favourite book or playing
with friends.

How can I tell if someone is happy?

When someone is happy, they may smile and laugh a lot. They may talk a lot, too.

Happy people can be a lot of fun to be around. They may be full of **energy**!

Can I join in when someone is happy?

It is great to share in someone's happiness! Tell them that you are happy that they are happy.

Ask them if you can join in the fun.
If they say no, that's OK. They may
just feel like being quietly happy on
their own.

19

Enjoy feeling happy!

We all have different **feelings** at different times. Enjoy your happiness! Try to share it with others, too.

If you feel sad or angry, think about happy times. Remember, you can soon feel happy again.

What are these feelings?

A

B

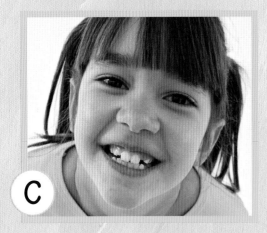

C

D

Which of these people look happy?

What are the other people feeling?

Look at page 24 to see the answer.

Picture glossary

energy
when you do not feel even
a little bit tired, you have
a lot of energy

feeling
something that you feel
inside. Happiness is
a feeling.

grinning
smiling a big smile

Index

Answers to the questions on page 22

The person in picture C looks happy. The other people could be angry, sad, or jealous.

Note to Parents and Teachers

Reading for information is an important part of a child's literacy development. Learning begins with a question about something. Help children think of themselves as investigators and researchers by encouraging their questions about the world around them. Most chapters in this book begin with a question. Read the question together. Look at the pictures. Talk about what you think the answer might be. Then read the text to find out if your predictions were correct. Think of other questions you could ask about the topic, and discuss where you might find the answers. Assist children in using the picture glossary and the index to practice new vocabulary and research skills.